SALE
OF BOOKS

AFTER
SCHOOL
3.30 p.m.
ON
TUESDAY

LOST
PROPERTY
SEE THE
CARETAKER

Caretaker

CHOIR
PRACTICE
FRIDAY
ROOM 3
At 3.15

JUMBO
JUMBLE SALE
PLEASE BRING
DONATIONS TO
THE STAFF
ROOM

First published 2005 by Walker Books Ltd
87 Vauxhall Walk, London SE11 5HJ

2 4 6 8 10 9 7 5 3 1

Text © 2005 David Wood   Illustrations © 2000, 2005 Jill Barton

David Wood and Jill Barton have asserted their moral rights.

This book has been typeset in Stempel Schneidler

Printed and bound in Great Britain by CPD (Wales), Ebbw Vale.

British Library Cataloguing in Publication Data: a catalogue record for this
book is available from the British Library

ISBN 0-7445-8397-7

www.walkerbooks.co.uk

LADY LOLLIPOP

A PLAY FOR CHILDREN

From the book by **Dick King-Smith**

Adapted by **David Wood**

Illustrated by **Jill Barton**

WALKER BOOKS
AND SUBSIDIARIES
LONDON · BOSTON · SYDNEY · AUCKLAND

TOYS FOR AFRICA
ANY UNWANTED
TOYS ROOM 5
Thank you

To the children of
Louth Kidgate Primary School,
Partney C of E Primary School,
Withern St Margaret's C of E Primary School,
Willoughby St Helena's C of E Primary School,
Saltfleetby C of E Primary School and
North Cockerington C of E Primary School,
whose workshops on Lady Lollipop *helped*
so much in bringing the story from page to stage

And to
Gail Rhodes, Rob Ashton, Sharon Humphreys,
Jane Salt and Ned Pickerill
who offered such effective experience and leadership

Thank you all
D. W.

A word from Dick King-Smith...

I expect you can imagine how thrilled I was when I heard that my friend David Wood was going to adapt another book of mine for the stage. (I say "another", because he had already done a wonderful adaptiation of *Babe*.) This story is also about a pig, a pig called Lollipop, who belongs to a very spoiled little princess. Thanks to her, the princess becomes a lot nicer by the end of the play.

I was a teacher once, many years ago, and when I showed the draft of this play to the head of that very school at which I had taught, she was mad keen for the children to perform it. Could they, she asked me?

Could they, I asked David?

To cut a long story short, they could and they did.

So the day came when David Wood and I sat side by side in the hall of Farmborough Primary School, near Bath, and watched the World Premiere of the play called *Lady Lollipop*, and what fun it was!

Every child in the school had a part, and how well they played them! Princess Penelope, her father King Theophilus, her mother Queen Ethelwynne, Penelope's friend Johnny Skinner the gardener, the palace servants, the pig-keepers, the pigs – everyone enjoyed themselves tremendously.

And so did I!

And a word from David Wood...

It has been great fun adapting Dick King-Smith's warm and funny story into this play version.

I wanted to have *lots* of parts, so that *lots* of children can be involved. It should be ideal for a class of thirty to perform, but by increasing the number of Pig-keepers or Roses or Palace Staff, more classes – even the whole school – can be in it.

Hopefully the play has something interesting for everyone to do. The main actors, like Princess Penelope or Johnny Skinner, have lots to say and therefore to remember, others, like the Palace Staff, have less, and some are completely silent.

The play is simple to stage. You need only an open space, a few props and two thrones. By having the Palace Staff act as stage managers as well as narrators, scene changes should be simple too. At the back of the book there are notes about this, as well as tips on music, mime, props and costumes.

And of course you don't need to put the play on at all. You can just read it. Out loud with others, or on your own to yourself.

Whatever you do, I hope you enjoy your-selves very, very much!

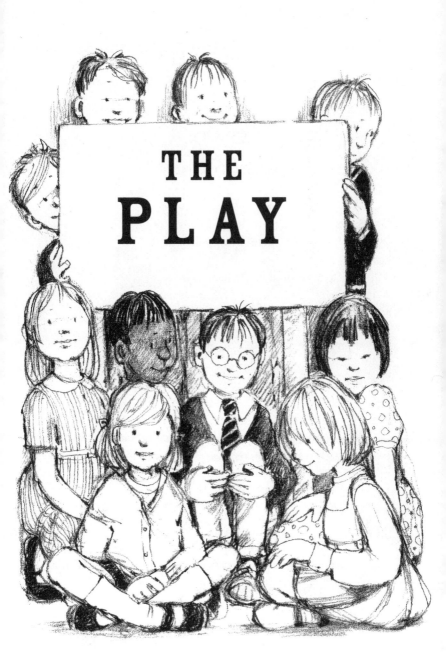

THE
PLAY

CHARACTERS

On stage:

PALACE STAFF (6) – *efficient and formal*

KING THEOPHILUS – *hearty and friendly*

QUEEN ETHELWYNNE – *sometimes a bit fierce*

PRINCESS PENELOPE – *spoiled and rude (at first)*

PIG-KEEPERS (5) – *rural, respectful*

PIGS (5) – *untrained, noisy*

JOHNNY SKINNER – *clever, modest, kind*

LOLLIPOP – *bright, well-trained*

ROSES (8) – *neglected (at first)*

FLOWER SHOW JUDGE – *enthusiastic*

Off stage:

MUSICIANS

Extra stage managers, prompter, costume and prop assistants

LIST OF SCENES

Note: Two thrones – in changing positions – are all that is needed to suggest where each scene takes place. The locations are written on signs attached to the thrones. See pp. 58–9 for more about this.

Scene 1   THE THRONE ROOM

[*Two thrones are centre-stage*]

MUSICIANS: [*Fanfare*]

[*Enter* PALACE STAFF. *They stand formally either side of the two thrones*]

PALACE STAFF 1: Once upon a time…

PALACE STAFF 2: In a faraway land…

PALACE STAFF 3: There lived a little princess.

MUSICIANS: [*A pounding percussion beat*]

[*Enter* PRINCESS PENELOPE *stomping crossly to centre-stage. She stands, looking fierce*]

PALACE STAFF 4: She was a very spoiled child.

PALACE STAFF 5: Her mother, Queen Ethelwynne…

MUSICIANS: [*Short fanfare*]

[*Enter* QUEEN *graciously. She sits on her throne*]

PALACE STAFF 5: …spoiled her quite a bit.

[*The* QUEEN *takes a marshmallow from a bag and gives it to* PRINCESS PENELOPE, *who stuffs it in her mouth*]

PALACE STAFF 6: Her father, King Theophilus…

MUSICIANS: [*Short fanfare*]

[*Enter* KING *grandly. He sits on his throne*]

PALACE STAFF 1: ...spoiled her rotten.

> [*The* KING *goes to take a marshmallow from a bag, then hands the bag to* PENELOPE, *who greedily stuffs lots in her mouth*]

ALL PALACE STAFF: The Palace Staff agreed that Princess Penelope was a RIGHT PAIN IN THE NECK.

> [*The* PALACE STAFF, *embarrassed by their lack of restraint, resume their formal poses*]

KING and QUEEN: Penelope!

PENELOPE: [*Rudely, spluttering and spraying marshmallow*] What d'you want?

QUEEN: Now, now.

KING: Steady on, old girl.

KING and QUEEN: We want to ask you something.

PENELOPE: What?

QUEEN: Soon it will be your birthday.

KING: What would you like for a present?

QUEEN: A pony?

PENELOPE: Don't like horses.

KING: A puppy then?

PENELOPE: Don't like dogs.

QUEEN: Or a kitten?

PENELOPE: Don't like cats.

KING: Well, you tell us, darling. What *would* you like?

PENELOPE: A pig.

KING and QUEEN: What!

PENELOPE: I want a pig for a pet.

QUEEN: A pig, Penelope? But a pig is a dirty animal.

PENELOPE: Is not!

KING: A pig is an ugly beast.

PENELOPE: Is not!

KING and QUEEN: A pig is a stupid creature.

PENELOPE: Is not! I wanna pig, I wanna pig, I WANNA PIG!!!
     [*She looks challengingly at her parents*]

KING: [*With a sigh*] All right, then, my sweet. Daddy will buy
     you a pig.

QUEEN: Aaaaaaaaaaaaaagh!

[*She faints into the* KING's *arms.* PENELOPE *smiles triumphantly*]

MUSICIANS: [*A handbell rings*]

>[*The* PALACE STAFF *step in front of the thrones and, reading from scrolls, give a proclamation*]

PALACE STAFF 1: Calling all keepers of pigs!

ALL PALACE STAFF: Calling all keepers of pigs!

PALACE STAFF 1: From North, from South,

PALACE STAFF 2: From East, from West,

PALACE STAFF 3: Pig-keepers all,

PALACE STAFF 4: By Royal request,

PALACE STAFF 5: Please bring one pig,

PALACE STAFF 6: The pick of your sty,

PALACE STAFF 1: To the palace next Monday!

>[*The* PALACE STAFF *let their scrolls roll up, cease the formal proclamation and talk more confidentially to the audience*]

MUSICIANS: [*Rhythmic accompaniment*]

ALL PALACE STAFF: And this is why:
It's the Princess's birthday
And she wants a pet.
So of course a pet

She is going to get.
But she doesn't want a cat
Or a dog or a rat.
Between you and me
The Princess is a brat.
Princess Penelope wants a pig!
It's not a joke, she wants a pig!
So Pig-keepers all,
This is the news –
Bring a pig to the Palace
So the Princess can choose.

MUSICIANS: [*The rhythm changes to a marching beat*]

[*The* PALACE STAFF *back upstage to either side of the thrones as the* KING *and* QUEEN *stand and move to one side, where* PRINCESS PENELOPE *joins them*]

[*Some of the* PALACE STAFF *exit. Others turn the thrones outward to reveal "Great Park" on the sides, leaving a space like a gateway. They stand like sentries as the* PIG-KEEPERS *and their* PIGS *enter through the gateway. They stand in a line.* JOHNNY SKINNER *and* LOLLIPOP *are at the end*]

Scene 2   THE GREAT PARK

[*The* PIGS *all grunt loudly*]

QUEEN: Theophilus, do I have to be here with all these ugly, dirty, stupid creatures?

KING: Of course, Ethelwynne. It's Penelope's birthday. Good morning, Pig-keepers!

PIG-KEEPERS: [*Muttering*] Mornin', sir.

KING: Er … good morning, pigs.

PIGS: [*Grunt*]

KING: Now, Penelope, which pig would you prefer?
[*The Royal party start walking down the line*]

PIG-KEEPER 1: My pig's called Spotty, miss. 'Cos of his spots.
[PENELOPE *looks at the pig and makes her decision*]

PENELOPE: No!

PIG-KEEPER 2: My pig's called Droopy, miss. 'Cos of his ears.

PENELOPE: No!

PIG-KEEPER 3: My pig's called Curly, miss. 'Cos of his tail.

PENELOPE: No!

PIG-KEEPER 4: My pig's called Porky, miss. 'Cos he's … porky.

PENELOPE: No!

PIG-KEEPER 5: My pig's called Perky, miss. 'Cos he's always falling asleep.

PIG 5: [*Loud snore*]

PIG-KEEPER 5: Perky. It's a joke.

PENELOPE: No!

> [*They come to the last pig-keeper and pig –* JOHNNY SKINNER *and* LOLLIPOP]

PENELOPE: Want THAT one!

> [*The* QUEEN *gasps in horror*]

KING: But darling, you can't have that one. It's the scruffiest, ugliest pig of the lot.

PENELOPE: Is NOT!

JOHNNY: You're right, miss. You've picked the best one. Scruffy and ugly she may be, like your dad says, but she's the brightest, cleverest pig you ever did see. Just watch this.

> [*He brings* LOLLIPOP *forward*]

Sit!

> [LOLLIPOP *sits*]

Down!

> [LOLLIPOP *lies down*]

Roll over!

> [LOLLIPOP *rolls over*]

Stand!

    [LOLLIPOP *stands*]

PIG-KEEPERS: Will you look at that!

    [*They clap*]

PIGS: [*Grunts of amazement and approval*]

JOHNNY: I trained her myself, miss. I shall be ever so sorry to see her go. She's all I've got.

QUEEN: You must have a mother and father, haven't you?

JOHNNY: No, ma'am, I'm an orphan.

PENELOPE: Oh well, don't worry. Daddy will get you another pig.

    [*She brings* LOLLIPOP *forward*]

Sit!

    [LOLLIPOP *stays standing.* PENELOPE *stamps her foot*]

SIT!

    [LOLLIPOP *stays standing*]

KING: Choose another pig, Penelope my love. This creature only obeys the boy.

PENELOPE: [*Hands on hips, quietly determined*] I … want … this … pig.

KING: Oh. [*To* JOHNNY] Sorry. She wants your one.

JOHNNY: Could I come and see her, now and again? The pig, I mean? [*He turns to* PENELOPE] Could I, miss, please?

[*Suddenly* LOLLIPOP *sits and looks appealingly up at* PENELOPE]

MUSICIANS: [*A magical "ting" from a triangle*]

[*Unexpectedly* PENELOPE *smiles*]

PENELOPE: What's your name?

JOHNNY: Johnny, miss, Johnny Skinner.

PENELOPE: All right, Johnny Skinner. You can be my personal pig-keeper. You can go on looking after this pig, which is now *my* pig, my birthday pig. Understood?

JOHNNY: Yes, miss.

QUEEN: But darling…

KING: But Penelope…

PENELOPE: But nothing. Come on, Johnny. [*They start to walk off.* PENELOPE *stops.* JOHNNY *and* LOLLIPOP *stop*] By the way, what's her name, this pig of mine?

JOHNNY: Well, miss. It's a bit of a strange name really, but it's what I've always called her.

PENELOPE: What is it?

JOHNNY: Lollipop.

[*All except* JOHNNY, LOLLIPOP *and* PENELOPE *(who freeze),
laugh heartily at the name.* PIG-KEEPERS *guffaw,* PIGS *grunt,
even the* PALACE STAFF *giggle and the* KING *and* QUEEN *smile.
During the laughter, the* PALACE STAFF *on-stage usher the* PIG-
KEEPERS *and their* PIGS *out of the gateway. All exit, laughing*]

MUSICIANS: [*Music as all exit*]

[*The* PALACE STAFF *turn the thrones to reveal the words
"Palace Stables" on the back, then exit*]

[JOHNNY, LOLLIPOP *and* PENELOPE *unfreeze. They are in the
Palace Stables*]

Scene 3   THE PALACE STABLES

PALACE STAFF 1: Later that day…

PALACE STAFF 2: In the Palace Stables.

[*They exit*]

PENELOPE: Lollipop? [*She smiles*] I like it. It's a nice name. But
why is she so thin? Don't you feed her properly?

JOHNNY: I've no money to buy food for her.

PENELOPE: What's she been eating then?

JOHNNY: Whatever she could find on the rubbish heaps, miss.

21

PENELOPE: We'll have to do something about that. [*Calling*] Daddy!

MUSICIANS: [*Lively percussion music*]

[*Enter the* KING. PENELOPE *whispers meaningfully in his ear. He thinks, then nods, and, with an expansive gesture, summons the* PALACE STAFF]

[*This scene could be fun using speeded-up action, like a silent film: enter two* PALACE STAFF *with plates of tasty scraps and leftovers for* LOLLIPOP *to tuck into. Enter two more bringing a scrubbing brush, soap, a sponge and a shampoo bottle. They vigorously mime cleaning* LOLLIPOP *as she mimes eating. Two more* PALACE STAFF *hurry on and dress* JOHNNY *in a royal apron and* LOLLIPOP *in a colourful collar. After this speedy action, the* PALACE STAFF *exit with all their props, leaving* LOLLIPOP *and* JOHNNY *transformed.* PRINCESS PENELOPE *has watched, pleased*]

[*As the percussion music stops, enter the* KING *carrying* PENELOPE'S *birthday cake, with eight candles. Some small pieces have already been cut*]

KING: Happy birthday, darling!

[PENELOPE *snatches the cake. The* KING *exits, rather miffed that he has received no thanks.* PENELOPE *greedily eats a piece, then thinks to offer* JOHNNY *some*]

PENELOPE: Johnny?

JOHNNY: Thanks, miss.

> [*He takes a piece and eats*]

PENELOPE: Lollipop?

> [*She picks up a piece and offers it to* LOLLIPOP]

LOLLIPOP: [*Shakes her head and grunts "no"*]

JOHNNY: She'd rather have a candle, miss.

PENELOPE: Oh. Very well. [*She offers a candle to* LOLLIPOP, *who happily eats it*] Johnny, you shouldn't really call me "miss".

JOHNNY: Why not, miss?

PENELOPE: Because you should address me as "Your Royal Highness".

JOHNNY: Oh.

PENELOPE: But actually, I don't mind. Have some more cake.

JOHNNY: [*Taking a piece*] Thanks, miss.

> [*He eats.* PENELOPE *eats a piece too.* LOLLIPOP *grunts meaningfully*]

PENELOPE: Oh. Sorry, Lollipop.

> [*She gives her another candle.* LOLLIPOP *eats it*]
> [PENELOPE *puts down the plate*]

Now, Lollipop…

> [*She strokes* LOLLIPOP]

Sit!

   [LOLLIPOP *stays standing*]

Sit!

   [LOLLIPOP *stays standing*]

SIT!

   [LOLLIPOP *stays standing*]

PENELOPE: [*Crossly to* JOHNNY] Why won't she do what I tell her? Everyone else does what I tell them. Why won't my pig?

JOHNNY: It's early days, miss. She's only ever been used to me.

PENELOPE: Well, she's not yours any longer. And don't you forget it!

   [*She flounces out*]

JOHNNY: Don't worry, Lollipop. [*He rubs the roots of* LOLLIPOP's *ears affectionately*] It's not really her fault. It's her dad and mum's fault for letting her have everything she wants. She was quite nice, wasn't she, when we were eating the cake?

LOLLIPOP: [*Grunts in agreement*]

JOHNNY: But the moment she couldn't get her own way, she flew off the handle, didn't she?

LOLLIPOP: [*Grunts in agreement*]

JOHNNY: I've been quite successful at training you. I wonder if I could train her?

LOLLIPOP: [*Shakes her head and grunts*]

JOHNNY: Fancy another candle?

LOLLIPOP: [*Nods her head and grunts enthusiastically*]
[*JOHNNY gives her one. She gobbles it up*]

MUSICIANS: [*Music to suggest "going to bed" time*]
[*Enter some of the PALACE STAFF. They turn thrones to face the front, then exit*]
[*JOHNNY (carrying the cake) and LOLLIPOP exit as the KING and QUEEN enter and sit on their thrones. The QUEEN has some roses which she arranges in a bowl held by the KING*]
[*PRINCESS PENELOPE enters too, looking fierce. Perhaps she plays a cup-and-ball game*]
[*Some of the PALACE STAFF remain, standing in attendance*]

Scene 4   THE THRONE ROOM

[*The music stops*]

PALACE STAFF 3: That evening…

PALACE STAFF 4: In the Throne Room.

QUEEN: Bedtime, Penelope.

PENELOPE: No.

QUEEN: Tell her, Theo.

KING: Come on, Penelope, old girl. You've had a long day.
You must be tired.

PENELOPE: Am NOT. I don't want to go to bed yet. It's my
birthday.

QUEEN: Yes, and you've had lots of presents, including a very
special one from Daddy. Not many little girls get given
a pig for a birthday present. And I haven't heard you thank-
ing him yet. How about saying, "Thank you, Daddy" now?

PENELOPE: Shan't. Not unless you let me stay up late.

KING: She could, couldn't she, Eth? Just this once? Just for a
treat?

QUEEN: Oh, I wash my hands of it. [*She crossly arranges roses*]

PENELOPE: Till midnight, Daddy?

KING: Well, all right then. Just this once.

PENELOPE: [*Smiling a self-satisfied smile*] Thanks. For the pig, I
mean.

KING: I'm glad you like it, darling. I'm sure it's very
comfortable in the Palace Stables.

PENELOPE: Oh, you needn't think it's going to stay there for ever.

QUEEN: [*Looking up*] What do you mean?

PENELOPE: My pig is going to be a house-pig. Or I suppose I should say a palace-pig.

QUEEN: A pig in the Palace? Aaaaaaaaaagh! Aaaaaaaaaagh!
[*She throws all the roses over the* KING *and exits screaming. The* KING *follows, trying to calm her*]

MUSICIANS: [*Quiet percussion music*]
[*The* PALACE STAFF *clear the roses and the bowl, then turn the thrones so that the words "Rose-garden" become visible with a gap left between the thrones to act as an entrance*]
[*Eight* ROSES *enter, with gloomy faces, and stand in a spaced cluster centre-stage*]

SCENE 5   THE ROSE-GARDEN

PALACE STAFF 5: Next day, Johnny and Lollipop explored the Palace grounds.

PALACE STAFF 6: They found the Queen's Rose-garden.
[*The* PALACE STAFF *disappear as* JOHNNY *and* LOLLIPOP *enter through the thrones.* JOHNNY *looks with interest at the* ROSES *as he and* LOLLIPOP *wander among them*]

27

[*As the music stops, the* QUEEN *enters crossly with a watering can. The* KING *follows trying to calm her*]

JOHNNY: [*Seeing the* QUEEN, *whispers*] Quick, Lollipop, hide.
[*They run to one side*]

KING: Eth, please, be reasonable.

QUEEN: I am being perfectly reasonable, Theo. If that ugly, dirty, stupid animal sets trotter inside the Palace, then out I go. There isn't room for both of us.
[JOHNNY *and* LOLLIPOP *look at each other*]

KING: But my dear Eth, we have two hundred and forty rooms in this Palace.

QUEEN: Which is not going to be turned into a pigsty.
[*The* KING *exits, defeated*]
[*The* QUEEN *starts watering the* ROSES]

MUSICIANS: [*A brief percussion tinkle each time she waters*]
[*When watered, each* ROSE *smiles weakly, stretches a little, then resumes its original unhealthy expression*]
[JOHNNY *indicates to* LOLLIPOP *to follow him. Unseen by the* QUEEN, *they creep towards the entrance. They nearly escape, but* LOLLIPOP *grunts*]

QUEEN: What's that? Who's there?

[*She turns.* JOHNNY *manages to push* LOLLIPOP *behind a throne, but is himself caught in the entrance*]

JOHNNY: It's me, ma'am. Johnny.

QUEEN: Is that ugly, dirty, stupid animal with you?

JOHNNY: You mean Lollipop, ma'am? Oh no, ma'am. Lollipop's in the Palace Stables.

QUEEN: And what are you doing, nosing in my Rose-garden?

JOHNNY: Roses are my favourite flowers, ma'am.

QUEEN: Really?

JOHNNY: Yes, ma'am. What variety are these? Are they hybrid teas or floribundas?

QUEEN: [*Softening*] They are a new hybrid, grown especially for me. They are called "Ethelwynne's Beautiful"!

JOHNNY: How true, ma'am.

QUEEN: [*Smiling, flattered*] Really?

JOHNNY: Oh, yes.

QUEEN: Roses are my favourite flowers too.

JOHNNY: Yes, ma'am?

QUEEN: I'm never happier than when I'm picking them or pruning them or dead-heading them. But they look so sad today. I fear I've neglected them, what with all this pig nonsense…

JOHNNY: Sorry, ma'am.

QUEEN: Oh, it's not your fault. Penelope is always so troublesome and time-consuming. But I've entered my roses in the local flower show and I so want them to be at their best.

JOHNNY: Yes, ma'am.

QUEEN: [*Turning fierce again*] So, Johnny, just make sure your … Penelope's ugly, dirty, stupid pig doesn't get in my Rose-garden. [*She starts to exit*] Just think of the chaos it could cause, the damage it could do…

[*Exit* QUEEN. JOHNNY *looks thoughtful. He has an idea*]

MUSICIANS: [*An idea "ting" from a triangle*]

JOHNNY: Lollipop! Lollipop!

[LOLLIPOP *appears round the throne and trots to* JOHNNY]
Look, Lollipop.

[*He points beneath one of the* ROSES]
The earth's all hard. The poor old roses' roots can't breathe. Please, turn the earth over with your snout. Rootle, Lollipop. Rootle!

MUSICIANS: [*Rootling music*]

> [*JOHNNY watches as LOLLIPOP rootles round each ROSE with her snout. As she progresses, each ROSE reacts with pleasure, shaking and stretching and smiling ecstatically*]
>
> [*The KING appears in the entrance. He watches, impressed*]
>
> [*When she has finished, LOLLIPOP returns to JOHNNY and the music stops*]

JOHNNY: Good pig! What a good pig!

> [*He rubs between LOLLIPOP's ears*]
>
> [*The KING hurries up to them*]

KING: Amazing! Astonishing! Brilliant, Johnny!

JOHNNY: Thank you, sir. But it wasn't really me.

KING: You've trained this ugly creature to rootle! How? Pigs are stupid!

> [*He looks at LOLLIPOP who looks meaningfully up into the eyes of the KING. Both freeze*]

MUSICIANS: [*A magical "ting" from a triangle*]

> [*The KING and LOLLIPOP look intently at each other*]
>
> [*Enter to one side quickly, PALACE STAFF 5 and 6*]

PALACE STAFF 5: The King stared into those eyes, fringed with long white lashes and shining with intelligence.

PALACE STAFF 6: He saw, looking back at him, someone not so very different from himself.

[PALACE STAFF *exit*]

KING: Ahhh … Lollipop! I apologize for calling you stupid. The Queen's roses have never looked happier! She'll be delighted!

[*The* ROSES *smile even more*]

[*Turning serious*] But, Lollipop, she'll never allow you inside the Palace. And Penelope insists you *live* in the Palace. But that's impossible.

JOHNNY: Why, sir?

KING: Oh, Johnny, don't you see? Lollipop's not er … Palace-trained. She'll, you know, do things…

JOHNNY: What things, sir?

KING: You know, do … her *business*. On the carpet! Messes. Everywhere!

JOHNNY: That's no problem, sir.

KING: No problem? The Queen will go potty!

JOHNNY: But, sir, look… [*Calling*] Lollipop!

[LOLLIPOP *turns and listens*]

Busy! [*Pause*] Busy, Lollipop! Busy.

MUSICIANS: [*Music for tension*]

> [LOLLIPOP *slowly turns, walks to a* ROSE, *squats and…*]
> MUSICIANS: [*A loud raspberry noise*]
> [*The* ROSE *reacts with excited pleasure to* LOLLIPOP'*s "business"*]
> [LOLLIPOP *returns to* JOHNNY *and the* KING]

KING: Astounding! She … performed on command! What a good pig!

JOHNNY: And her "business" will be good for Her Majesty's roses, sir.

KING: Indeed it will. [*Thoughtfully*] So Lollipop *is* Palace-trained.

JOHNNY: Yes sir. She could move in tomorrow!

KING: Mmmmm. [*Sudden thought*] But she'd bring a lot of muck in on her feet, wouldn't she? Mud everywhere?

JOHNNY: No, sir. Watch this. [*To* LOLLIPOP] Lollipop, wipe feet!
> [LOLLIPOP *walks forward and wipes her feet*]

KING: Extraordinary. What a good pig!

JOHNNY: And she could go in and out of the Palace whenever she wants, if you could get the Palace Carpenters to make a pig-flap for the door.

KING: A pig-flap! Johnny, you're a genius! I'll see to it at once. [*He starts to go. Suddenly he stops*] No, hang on. Lollipop may do all this for you, but will she do it for Penelope?

JOHNNY: Yes sir, if I train her.

KING: Train who? Lollipop or Penelope?

JOHNNY: Both of 'em, sir, if you like.

KING: Really? [*Thoughtfully*] Tell me, Johnny, would you say that my daughter is a bit spoiled?

JOHNNY: No.

KING: Oh.

JOHNNY: I'd say she is very spoiled indeed. She needs to be taught to think more about other people and less about herself.

KING: Mmm. Could you teach her, d'you think?

JOHNNY: I might be able to.

KING: If you can, Johnny, I'll reward you royally! Now, pig-flap. I must visit the Palace Carpenters. [*He moves off*]

JOHNNY: [*Calling after him*] And I'll keep Lollipop working on these roses, sir.

KING: Excellent, yes. You do that, you do that!

[*The* KING *exits*]

JOHNNY: But first, Lollipop… [LOLLIPOP *looks at him.*] We've got to train the Princess.

LOLLIPOP: [*Grunts a "yes"*]

MUSICIANS: [*Lively music*]
> [JOHNNY *and* LOLLIPOP *sit downstage as some* PALACE STAFF *enter and turn the thrones round so their backs face the audience, saying "Palace Stables". At the same time, the* ROSES *exit*]
> [*The music stops*]

Scene 6   THE PALACE STABLES

PALACE STAFF 1: Next morning…

PALACE STAFF 2: In the Palace Stables.
> [*They disappear behind the thrones as* PENELOPE *enters*]

PENELOPE: Morning, Johnny. Morning, Lollipop.
> [JOHNNY *stands*]

JOHNNY: Morning, miss. Lollipop, stand!
> [LOLLIPOP *stands*]

PENELOPE: The straw seems to be very clean. Have you just mucked out?

JOHNNY: No, miss. No need for that. You just watch.

> [*He leads* LOLLIPOP *to the side where we imagine the door to be. He points outside*]

Lollipop, busy!

> [LOLLIPOP *trots out of sight.* JOHNNY *and* PENELOPE *look off-stage*]

MUSICIANS: [*Loud raspberry sound*]

> [LOLLIPOP *returns and looks at* JOHNNY]

JOHNNY: Well done, Lollipop. What a good pig!

PENELOPE: That's brilliant, Johnny! She's Palace-trained!

JOHNNY: Yes, miss. And she's making your mother's roses happy too!

PENELOPE: [*To* LOLLIPOP, *rather fiercely*] Busy!

> [LOLLIPOP *looks surprised*]

PENELOPE: Busy!

LOLLIPOP: [*Grunts as if to say, "That's a silly instruction"*]

JOHNNY: No good saying that now, miss. She's only just done it.

PENELOPE: [*Getting cross*] Well, then, sit!

> [LOLLIPOP *stays standing*]

Why won't she do what I tell her? Stupid animal.

JOHNNY: Lollipop isn't stupid, miss. She just hasn't been trained to obey you, only me. But I might be able to train her to obey you too, if you would do something for me in return.

PENELOPE: Like what?

JOHNNY: Well, to begin with, you could speak more politely to Lollipop. Animals are very sensitive to the tone of people's voices. Try talking to her more gently, if you want her to obey you. [*He kneels down beside* LOLLIPOP] Go on, miss.

PENELOPE: [*More kindly*] Lollipop, sit!
    [LOLLIPOP *looks at* JOHNNY, *who nods. She sits*]
    She did it! I told her to do it and she did it! What next, Johnny?

JOHNNY: [*Standing up*] That's enough to begin with, miss.

PENELOPE: [*Losing her temper*] Is NOT! I want to make her do other things. Stand, Lollipop. STAND!
    [LOLLIPOP *stays sitting*]
    Do what I say!

LOLLIPOP: [*Grunts a refusal*]

JOHNNY: [*Quietly*] Lollipop, stand!
    [LOLLIPOP *stands*]

[*To* PENELOPE] You've got to learn to be more patient, you know, if you want your pig to obey you.

PENELOPE: How dare you!

JOHNNY: No good shouting at her and losing your temper.

PENELOPE: Listen to me…

JOHNNY: Trouble with you is, you always want to get your own way.

PENELOPE: I do not! I…
   [*She and* JOHNNY *are face to face*]
   [*Suddenly* LOLLIPOP *moves forward and looks* PENELOPE *in the eye. Both freeze*]

MUSICIANS: [*A magical "ting" from a triangle*]
   [*Enter, round the thrones, one each side,* PALACE STAFF 1 *and* 2]

PALACE STAFF 1: The Princess stared into those eyes, fringed with long white lashes and shining with intelligence.

PALACE STAFF 2: She saw, looking back at her, someone not so very different from herself.

BOTH: At that moment, though she herself didn't realize it, Princess Penelope grew up a little bit.
   [*The* PALACE STAFF *exit behind the thrones*]

[PENELOPE *suddenly smiles at* JOHNNY, *who smiles back*]

PENELOPE: All right, Johnny. I'll try to be more patient with both of you.

JOHNNY: That's good, miss.

LOLLIPOP: [*Grunts her agreement*]

PENELOPE: [*Gently*] Lollipop, sit!
    [LOLLIPOP *sits*]
  What a good pig! Lollipop, roll over!
    [LOLLIPOP *rolls over*]
  What a good pig!
    [*She holds out her hand*]
  Lollipop, shake.
    [LOLLIPOP *extends a trotter.* PENELOPE *shakes it*]
  Thank you, Lollipop.

JOHNNY: That's it, miss. Well done, miss.

PENELOPE: I wish you'd stop calling me "miss".

JOHNNY: But you said you didn't mind.

PENELOPE: I don't. But why don't you call me Penelope?

JOHNNY: All right, miss…
    [PENELOPE *looks at him*]
  I mean … Penelope.

[PENELOPE *holds out her hand.* JOHNNY *shakes it. Both smile. Both freeze*]

MUSICIANS: [*Extremely lively music*]

[*Enter the* PALACE STAFF, *running. They take up positions upstage, either side of the thrones. Two hold watering cans*]

Scene 7 THE PALACE STABLES AND THE ROSE-GARDEN

PALACE STAFF 1: The next few days were filled with feverish activity.

[*As in Scene 3, the action could be speeded up, like a silent film. Music would continue throughout*]

PALACE STAFF 2: Johnny trained Princess Penelope to train Lollipop.

[JOHNNY *mimes instructions to* PENELOPE, *who trains* LOLLIPOP. Sit. Stand. Roll over. Wipe feet. And again. Sit. Stand. Roll over. Wipe feet*]

[*As* JOHNNY *and* PENELOPE *shake hands and make a fuss of* LOLLIPOP, *the* ROSES *run in and take up their positions. The* PALACE STAFF *turn the thrones sideways to read "Rose-garden"*]

PALACE STAFF 3: In the Rose-garden, Johnny and Penelope watered the roses.

> [JOHNNY *and* PENELOPE *hurry to collect watering cans from the* PALACE STAFF, *and then run round watering the* ROSES]

PALACE STAFF 4: And Lollipop rootled them.

> [LOLLIPOP, *encouraged by* JOHNNY *and* PENELOPE, *runs from* ROSE *to* ROSE, *rootling*]
> [JOHNNY *and* PENELOPE *take their watering cans back to the* PALACE STAFF]

PALACE STAFF 5: And Lollipop was very, very busy.

> [*Encouraged by* JOHNNY *and* PENELOPE, LOLLIPOP *runs from* ROSE *to* ROSE *and squats to do her "business" under each one. The* ROSES *react delightedly*]

MUSICIANS: [*Over the continuing music, loud raspberry sounds accompany each "busy"*]

> [*After the first three "busys"…*]

PALACE STAFF 6: And the Palace Carpenters sawed and screwed and nailed a Royal pig-flap.

MUSICIANS: [*Over the continuing music and raspberry sounds, sawing and banging noises*]

> [*The music and activity build to a climax, then suddenly stop.* LOLLIPOP *is exhausted.* JOHNNY *and* PENELOPE *applaud her*]

PALACE STAFF 1: All was ready,

PALACE STAFF 2: All was set,

PALACE STAFF 3: To show the Queen

PALACE STAFF 4: That the Princess's pet

PALACE STAFF 5: Was Palace-trained,

PALACE STAFF 6: And therefore able

ALL PALACE STAFF: To say goodbye to the Palace Stables!

Scene 8   BEDTIME

[JOHNNY *and* PENELOPE *wave goodbye.* PENELOPE *exits. The* ROSES *and* PALACE STAFF *exit*]

MUSICIANS: [*A clock chimes midnight*]
[JOHNNY *and* LOLLIPOP *move downstage to one side, curl up and rest*]
[*As the chimes ring out, the* KING *and* QUEEN *enter sideways, holding a bedspread in front of them. This makes them appear to be in bed. They stand centre-stage*]
[*Two* PALACE STAFF *enter and stand either side of the "bed". As the chimes end…*]

PALACE STAFF 1: That night…

PALACE STAFF 2: In the Royal Bedchamber.

KING: Eth, dear.

QUEEN: [*Waking with a snort*] Yes, Theo.

KING: Tomorrow, Penelope has something to show us.

QUEEN: What?

KING: It's a secret.

QUEEN: Not tomorrow, Theo. It's the flower show, though my roses have little chance of winning.

KING: Penelope can show us her secret *before* the flower show.

QUEEN: Oh, very well.
[*They close their eyes*]

QUEEN: [*Suddenly opening her eyes*] Theo.

KING: [*Waking with a snort*] Yes, Eth.

QUEEN: That boy, Johnny, knows a lot about roses.

KING: Does he indeed, Eth?

QUEEN: Yes. He's not just a swineherd, he's a bright boy.

KING: Good, good.
[*They close their eyes*]

KING: [*Suddenly opening his eyes*] Eth.

QUEEN: [*Waking with a snort*] Yes, Theo.

KING: Lollipop is bright, too.

QUEEN: That pig? Don't imagine for one moment, Theophilus, that you can persuade me to change my mind and allow that ugly, dirty, stupid animal into my Palace.

KING: But...

QUEEN: No buts.
> [*They close their eyes. And start to snore*]

PALACE STAFF 1: The King and Queen...

PALACE STAFF 2: Fell asleep.
> [*Enter, sideways,* PENELOPE *holding a bedspread in front of her. On either side of her are* PALACE STAFF 3 *and* 4]

PALACE STAFF 3: In her bedchamber...

PALACE STAFF 4: Princess Penelope slept.
> [*All three stand to one side, opposite* JOHNNY *and* LOLLIPOP]
> [PALACE STAFF 5 *and* 6 *enter behind* JOHNNY *and* LOLLIPOP]

PALACE STAFF 5: And in the Palace Stables...

PALACE STAFF 6: Johnny and Lollipop slept.

ALL PALACE STAFF: They all began to dream...

MUSICIANS: [*Dreamy music*]

> [*Each dream is acted out in slow motion mime*]

PALACE STAFF 1: The Queen dreamed…

> [*The* QUEEN *opens her eyes*]

PALACE STAFF 2: That Lollipop was in the Palace.

> [LOLLIPOP *gets out of bed and enters the dream, approaching the* QUEEN *in bed*]
>
> [*The* QUEEN *mimes her horror at the pig approaching*]
>
> [LOLLIPOP *stretches up and puts her trotters on the bedspread, then pulls it to the floor. The Royal couple could be wearing funny night attire*]
>
> [LOLLIPOP *rootles the* QUEEN *out of bed and slowly chases her round*]
>
> [*Eventually the* QUEEN *goes back to bed and* PALACE STAFF 1 *and 2 rearrange the bedspread. The* QUEEN *closes her eyes*]
>
> [LOLLIPOP *returns to her position by* JOHNNY]

PALACE STAFF 2: The King dreamed…

> [*The* KING *opens his eyes*]

PALACE STAFF 1: Of having a well-behaved daughter with a well-behaved pig.

> [PRINCESS PENELOPE *slowly gets out of bed by creeping under the bedspread held by* PALACE STAFF 3 *and 4. She is met centre-stage by* LOLLIPOP. *Together, they slowly dance a few formal steps, like a minuet, before advancing to the* KING.

Then PENELOPE *performs a stately curtsey, and* LOLLIPOP *bows. The* KING *looks delighted]*

*[*PENELOPE *goes back to bed and* LOLLIPOP *returns to her position by* JOHNNY*]*

PALACE STAFF 5: Johnny dreamed…

*[*JOHNNY *slowly opens his eyes and stands]*

PALACE STAFF 6: That the Queen grew to love Lollipop.

*[*LOLLIPOP, *instructed by* JOHNNY, *trots slowly centre-stage, as the* QUEEN *opens her eyes and watches from bed]*

*[*LOLLIPOP *performs a slow rootle, then squats and is "busy"]*

MUSICIANS: *[Over the dreamy music, a long, deep raspberry]*

*[*LOLLIPOP *looks up at the* QUEEN, *who is delighted. She gets out of bed as the* PALACE STAFF *hold up the bedspread. The* QUEEN *enfolds* LOLLIPOP *in a warm embrace. Then they both return to their sleeping positions]*

PALACE STAFF 3: Princess Penelope dreamed…

*[*PENELOPE *opens her eyes]*

PALACE STAFF 4: She could train Lollipop…

[From her bed, PENELOPE *gestures to* LOLLIPOP, *who moves centre-stage]*

PALACE STAFF 3: To eat at table.

*[*LOLLIPOP *"sits" on her hind legs and eats delicately with her trotters]*

PALACE STAFF 4: And play the piano.

> [PENELOPE *gestures, and slowly* LOLLIPOP *mimes playing a complicated tune on the piano. Then she returns to her position by* JOHNNY]

PALACE STAFF 5: Lollipop, who was the star of everyone else's dream…

PALACE STAFF 6: Slept soundly and dreamed of … nothing.

> [LOLLIPOP *snores contentedly*]
> [*All sleep*]

MUSICIANS: [*The sudden sound of a cockerel crowing*]

> [*All wake up*]

MUSICIANS: [*Lively music*]

> [*Sudden activity. The* KING, QUEEN *and* PENELOPE *exit quickly, taking their bedspreads with them.* JOHNNY *and* LOLLIPOP *stay on stage as some of the* PALACE STAFF *fetch the pig-flap and position it on the thrones*]
> [*The* ROSES *enter and take up their positions*]

Scene 9 THE ROSE-GARDEN

PALACE STAFF 5: Next morning.

PALACE STAFF 6: Saturday, the day of the flower show.

[*Music continues as* JOHNNY *encourages* LOLLIPOP *to have a quick rootle round the* ROSES, *who react happily. This is interrupted by…*]

MUSICIANS: [*Fanfare*]

[*Enter* PENELOPE, *leading the* KING *and* QUEEN. JOHNNY *hides* LOLLIPOP. *The* PALACE STAFF *stand upstage*]

PENELOPE: This way, Mummy.

KING: Good morning, Johnny!

JOHNNY: Morning, sir, ma'am, miss … er, Penelope.

QUEEN: Now hurry up, Penelope. Show me whatever it is you wish to show me. I have the flower show to… [*She sees the* ROSES *who are smiling rapturously*] Oh! My roses! How beautifully happy they look!

PENELOPE: Yes, Mummy. And you know why?

QUEEN: Why?

PENELOPE: [*Calling*] Lollipop!

[LOLLIPOP *appears from behind* JOHNNY]

QUEEN: [*Horrified*] Aaagh! [*Angrily*] What is that ugly, dirty, stupid animal doing in my Rose-garden?

PENELOPE: That's what I want to show you. Watch. Lollipop, rootle!

48

MUSICIANS: [*Rootling music*]

> [LOLLIPOP *rootles round the* ROSES, *who react happily, then returns and looks up at* PENELOPE]

PENELOPE: What a good pig! Now, Lollipop, busy!

MUSICIANS: [*Lively music*]

> [LOLLIPOP *runs to three* ROSES, *squats and performs. The* ROSES *react even more happily*]

MUSICIANS: [*Three raspberries*]

> [LOLLIPOP *goes to the* QUEEN]

PENELOPE: Sit!

> [LOLLIPOP *sits and looks at the* QUEEN]

See, Mummy? Lollipop's been cultivating your Rose-garden. Johnny trained her and now he's trained me.

> [*The* QUEEN *looks at* LOLLIPOP. *Both freeze*]

MUSICIANS: [*A magical "ting" from a triangle*]

PALACE STAFF 3: The Queen stared into those eyes, fringed with long white lashes and shining with intelligence.

PALACE STAFF 4: She saw, looking back at her, someone not so very different from herself.

> [*All wait with bated breath*]

QUEEN: What a good pig!

> [*Everyone cheers*]

How can I thank you?

KING: Maybe, Eth, you could er ... invite her to breakfast.

QUEEN: [*Momentarily horrified*] Inside the Palace?

KING: Why not?

QUEEN: Why not?

PENELOPE: It's all right, Mummy, really. Look. Lollipop, wipe feet!

> [LOLLIPOP *energetically wipes her trotters*]

Good pig! Now ... pig-flap!

> [*All watch and clear a way for* LOLLIPOP]

MUSICIANS: [*Drum roll*]

> [LOLLIPOP *walks to the pig-flap and goes through it*]
> [*All cheer and clap*]
> [*The* QUEEN *smiles*]

PRINCESS: Please, Mummy, can Lollipop live in the Palace?

KING: Sounds fair to me, Eth. And Penelope asked very politely.

> [*Pause. All look at the* QUEEN]

QUEEN: Of course she can!

[*All cheer and clap*]

[LOLLIPOP *runs back through the pig-flap and sits by the* QUEEN]

And, Lollipop, will you please rootle my roses every day?

LOLLIPOP: [*Grunts "Yes"*]

[*Enter the* FLOWER SHOW JUDGE *with a large silver cup*]

JUDGE: Your Majesty, I'm delighted to inform you that your roses have won first prize in the flower show. Congratulations!

[*He presents her with the cup. All cheer. The* ROSES *look particularly pleased with themselves*]

QUEEN: Thank you. I'm thrilled! But really this belongs to Lollipop.

PENELOPE: And Johnny.

KING: She's right, Eth.

QUEEN: Where *is* Johnny?

[JOHNNY *who has been standing watching to one side, now comes forward*]

JOHNNY: Here, ma'am.

QUEEN: Johnny, how would you like to be my under-gardener? I could do with your expert help. And there is a cottage vacant for you to live in.

JOHNNY: Thank you, ma'am.

>[PRINCESS PENELOPE *comes happily to join* JOHNNY]

KING: Well done, Eth. And Johnny, for all you've done for us, especially Penelope, I'm jolly well going to make you a Duke!

>[*All cheer and clap*]

And as for Lollipop...

>[LOLLIPOP *trots forward*]

I'm jolly well going to make her a Lady!

>[*He presents* LOLLIPOP *with a medal*]

Lady Lollipop!

ALL: Lady Lollipop!

MUSICIANS: [*Jubilant fanfare*]

>[*All form a tableau and freeze for applause*]
>[*Then the* PALACE STAFF *step forward*]

PALACE STAFF 1: And the Palace Staff
>Are pleased to declare,

PALACE STAFF 2: Lollipop's brought a
>Breath of fresh air!

PALACE STAFF 3: Everyone's happy
>Discovering that

PALACE STAFF 4: No more is the Princess
A spoiled brat!

PALACE STAFF 5: Thanks to Duke Johnny
We all want to say,

PALACE STAFF 6: Long live Lady Lollipop!

ALL [*except* LOLLIPOP]: Hip, hip, hooray!

LOLLIPOP: [*Grunts*]

MUSICIANS: [*Happy music*]
[*Optional dance of celebration*]

THE END

CURTAIN CALL

STAGING IDEAS

SET

Simplicity is all! *Lady Lollipop: A Play for Children* can be staged with just two pieces of furniture. The two thrones can be turned different ways to create each scene – the locations, apart from the Throne Room, being signposted on the sides and back of them.

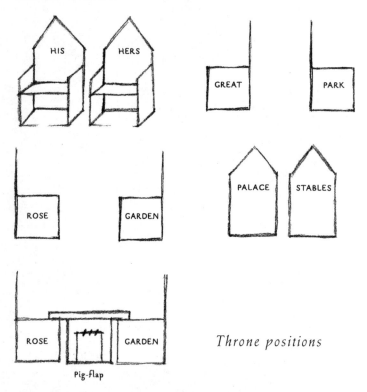

Throne positions

To make an area for the Rose-garden, it might be an idea to paint a circle centre stage.

You could hang curtains or painted canvas "flats" either

side to provide entrances and exits. No front curtains are necessary.

If you can hang a curtain at the back for the actors to walk behind, it might help when arranging entrances and exits. But this is by no means essential!

The musicians need to be able to see the actors, because they sometimes play music to fit their actions. So they should ideally sit in the front of the acting area, to one side.

As long as the acting area is well lit, you won't need any lighting changes.

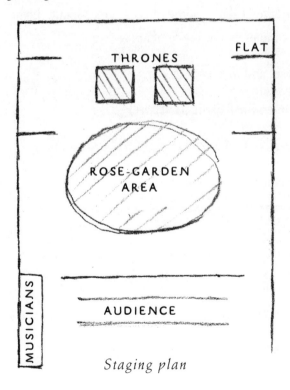

Staging plan

PROPS

Apart from the two thrones, the following props are needed:

2 bags of marshmallows (KING and QUEEN)

6 scrolls for the proclamation (PALACE STAFF)

Scrubbing brush, soap, sponge, shampoo bottle (PALACE STAFF)

Plate of leftovers (PALACE STAFF)

Birthday cake – some pieces already cut. Eight edible candles can be made of apple (KING)

Roses and rose-bowl (QUEEN)

Cup-and-ball game (PENELOPE)

3 watering cans (QUEEN, JOHNNY, PENELOPE)

Bedspread (KING and QUEEN)

Bedspread (PENELOPE)

Pig-flap – this sits on the arms of the thrones, with a hinged flap in a wooden frame.

Silver cup (FLOWER SHOW JUDGE)

Medal (KING for LOLLIPOP)

COSTUMES AND MASKS

Costumes could be complicated if you want them to be (have a look at Jill Barton's pictures in Dick King-Smith's original book to inspire you). Or they could be very simple. The whole cast could be dressed in jeans and t-shirts and wear just one or two identifying items:

The King, Queen and Penelope could wear paper crowns.

Johhny could wear a waistcoat. (In the play he is given a royal apron.)

The Palace Staff could wear sashes.

The Pigs could wear simple masks which don't cover their eyes or mouths, but give them ears and a snout. (In the play Lollipop is given a colourful collar.)

The Roses could wear gloves or "petal ruffs" round their necks.

The Pig-keepers could wear hats.

The Flower Show Judge could wear a rosette.

MUSIC

The music cues suggested in the playscript could all be played on percussion instruments.

It is fun trying out different sounds to fit the actions of the play. Different rhythms and tempos will suggest themselves and magic triangle "tings" and horn "raspberries" will help accompany the story.

Some teachers may want to use piano accompaniment to hold everything together but this should not be essential.

MIME AND MOVEMENT

In the play there are opportunities for slow motion (the dreams in scene 8) and for speeded-up action (feeding and cleaning Lollipop in scene 3 and rootling and training in scene 7). These are great fun, but also demand thoughtful timing and precision.

All the cast will gain confidence, as well as enjoyment, from initial movement sessions to find appropriate styles for the Pigs, for the Roses, and for the Palace Staff's formal, yet bustling, scene changing.

The formal movement of the Palace occupants should contrast with the casual movement of the Pig-keepers and the "tomboy" movement of the Princess. The Roses cannot move their feet, so will have to find an individual expressiveness in their head and body movements.

ACTING TIPS

Acting needs clarity of movement and diction. When finding your character, imagine a real person who moves and talks like the character you are playing, and try to imitate them.

Try to speak naturally, but with enough volume for the audience to hear you. If you use an accent, don't make it too broad in case it is hard to understand.

Acting is about team work. Listening to the other actors and reacting to their words is just as important as saying your own.

To tell the story well, every actor is important. It doesn't matter how many or how few lines you have to say or scenes you have to play, your part is as vital as everyone else's in making the audience understand and enjoy the play.

Dick King-Smith, a former dairy farmer, is one of the world's favourite children's book authors. He won the Guardian Fiction Award for *The Sheep-Pig* (filmed as *Babe*), was named Children's Book Author of the Year in 1991 and won the 1995 Children's Book Award for *Harriet's Hare*. His titles for Walker Books include the much-loved Sophie series, *Asristotle*, *Lady Lollipop* and its sequel, *Clever Lollipop*.

David Wood began writing as a student at Oxford University in the sixties. He wrote his first play for children in 1967 and has since written over fifty more. As well as acting on stage and screen, David has adapted many well-known books into stage plays, including Dick King-Smith's *The Sheep-Pig*, and Roald Dahl's *The BFG* and *The Witches*. He was recently awarded an OBE for services to literature and drama.

Jill Barton was Highly Commended for the 1993 Kate Greenaway medal for *The Pig in the Pond* (by Martin Waddell). The many other titles she has illustrated include *The Happy Hedgehog Band* and *Little Mo* (also by Martin Waddell), *What Baby Wants* and *Rattletrap Car* (by Phyllis Root), and seven Baby Duck stories (by Amy Hest). Jill lives in Devon and has three children.